# zion & zara stories
## the big bike race

written by: tenesha jarvis

illustrated by: gabriel curley

AuthorHouse™
1663 Liberty Drive
Bloomington, IN 47403
www.authorhouse.com
Phone: 1 (800) 839-8640

Published by AuthorHouse 10/19/2018

ISBN: 978-1-5462-6439-2 (sc)
ISBN: 978-1-5462-6440-8 (e)

Library of Congress Control Number: 2018912329

Print information available on the last page.

This book is printed on acid-free paper.

authorHOUSE®

Zion and Zara Hampton were born on August 23$^{rd}$ in Brooklyn, NY. They were only 10 years old, but they sure weren't your average 10-year olds.

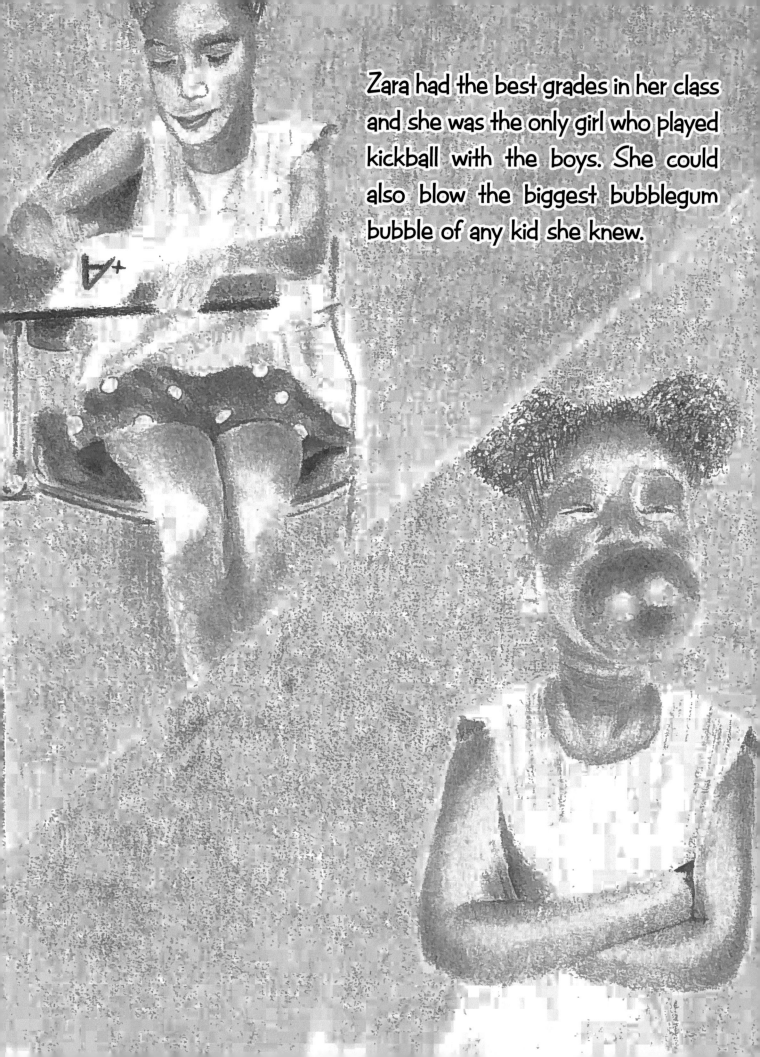

Zara had the best grades in her class and she was the only girl who played kickball with the boys. She could also blow the biggest bubblegum bubble of any kid she knew.

Zion was a lot like his sister. He did very well in school, he could play any sport (and play it well), and he was very protective of his twin sister.

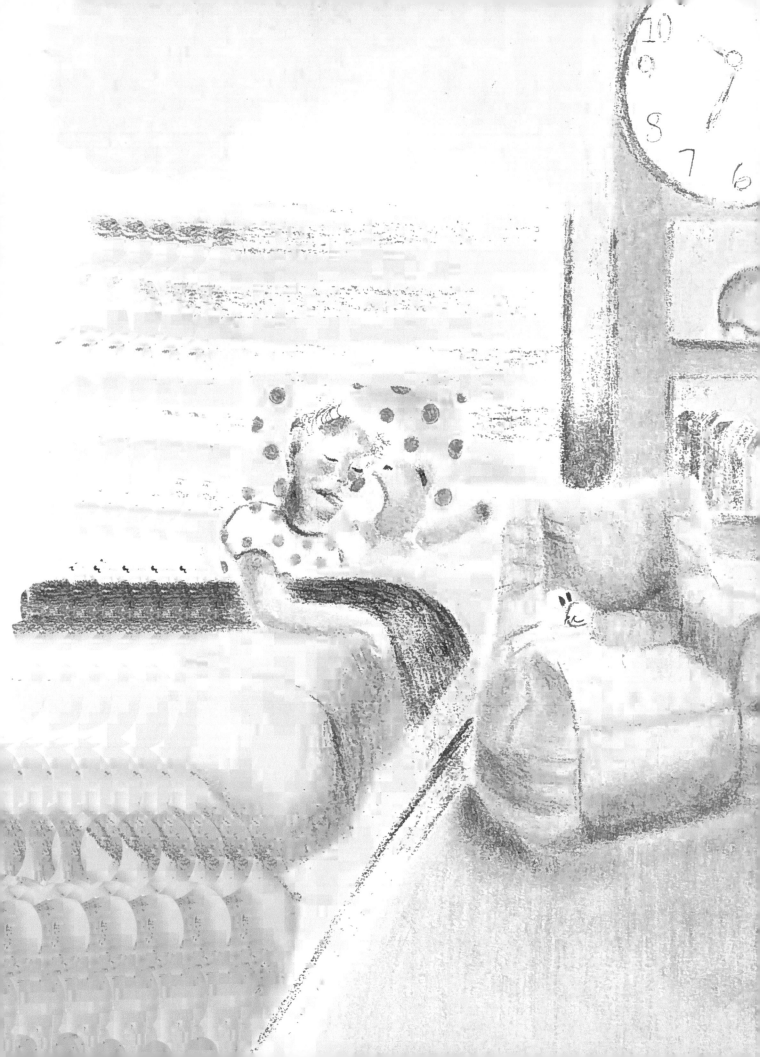

On this particular day, Zion and Zara were super excited because it was the first day of summer vacation. No more teachers, no more of that awful school lunch, and best of all, no more homework! It was also the day of the Big Bike Race!

Zion had been looking forward to this day all year. He jumped out of bed and ran to the window. He could see all the neighborhood kids already laughing, playing and preparing for the race.

"Everyone is already outside, Zara, we've got to hurry!", Zion yelled excitedly to his sister. Zara was already putting on her play clothes and heading for the front door.
"I don't know about you, Zion, but I'm ready!"

They crept down the stairs and out the front door to join their friends. They would surely be in trouble for not having breakfast first but they'd worry about that later.

"Hey, Zion! Hey Zara!", they heard Sammy shout from down the street as he walked over with Petey. "You guys ready for the big race? I've been training all year and I am ready to win!"

"Of course, I'm ready!", replied Zion, "I've even gotten a brand-new bike."

"What about you, Zara, are you excited about the race?", asked Petey, who lived just a few doors down from the twins.

"I won't be racing, but yes, I'm very excited! I'm excited to see my brother win with his brand-new bike", Zara replied.

The four friends walked up and down the street admiring the scene and all the different types of bicycles. There were bikes with ribbons, bows, and baskets. There were blue bicycles, pink bicycles, there were even bicycles with four or five colors. Those were Zara's favorite.

There were face painters, photo booths, and even a cotton candy machine. They all decided to stop and get a popsicle from the icee man to have and enjoy while they walked.

They soon found Jordan who was proudly shining her bicycle. It had flowers painted all over and purple tassels on the handlebars. There was even a bright pink bell. Zara loved it!

"Hey you guys!", said Jordan excitedly as they approached, "What do ya think about my bike? My Dad and I painted it together."
"It looks great!", replied Zara, "Are you going to use it in the race?"
"I sure am and I can't wait for everyone to see it.", said Jordan, "Hey Zion, where's your bike?"
"It's at my house. I'm waiting until the start of the race to bring it out.", replied Zion.

Just then, the announcer for the race called out on his megaphone, "ALL RACERS HAVE 5 MINUTES TO REPORT TO THE STARTING LINE"

Zion ran down to his house and soon returned with his new shiny, red bike. It had a bell, a matching helmet, and even really cool pegs like the big kids had. Not only was he ready to ride his new bike, he was ready to win with it too.

"Wow! That's the coolest bike I've ever seen!", exclaimed Jordan. "Thanks!", replied Zion as he stood nice and tall next to his bike. "Think it'll win the race?", she asked. "There's only one way to find out.", he said.

All of the kids lined their bikes up at the starting line and Zara made her way down to the finish line to cheer her brother on.

People were cheering and clapping on the sidelines, but the racers all seemed focused.

They all started revving their engines.
"Vroom...Vroom...Vroom"
"On Your Marks. Get Set. GO!", shouted the announcer.
And off they went.

FINISH

Zion could see Zara way down at the
end of the street.
"Go Zion! Go!" she was yelling and
waving her arms in the air.
But, he could also see Sammy. She
was just a couple of feet ahead of
him and Flora was right on his tail.

INISH

If he didn't pick up speed he would surely lose the race. So, that's exactly what he did.

458

178

He began to pedal as fast as he could.
He was pedaling so fast, he was sure he
could see smoke coming from his tires.
Soon he had passed Sammy and he left
Flora in his dust.

Before he knew it, Zara was in arm's reach and Zion crossed the finish line.

He hadn't noticed it at first, but he did it! He won the race! All his friends began to cheer and were giving out high fives.

"Zion, I've never seen someone ride a bicycle so fast! That was amazing!" said Zara excitedly.

"I know. It must be my brand-new bike." Zion said proudly, as they walked back to the starting line.

Zion won a shiny, gold, trophy and was the happiest kid ever. The only thing Zion and Zara could think was, "This is the perfect way to start the summer."

Printed in the United States
By Bookmasters